Georgie Henley is a poet with a bent for the embodied and breathlessly sensual. At turns wry and despairing, then full of yearning and thwarted desire, this pamphlet has many faces. Unafraid to be playful and straight up weird, Henley takes the reader on many delicious digressions.

Vanessa Kisuule

To read Georgie Henley's Amphibian *is to enter a space of mythic brightness. These are poems that ache on the page, that bare their strength through the visceral lyric. This is a thrilling debut, which illuminates fear, shame, sensuality, and love through poetry which asserts that 'time is told through our body'.*

Ella Duffy

Georgie Henley's poems are intricate, feminist, and embodied. They fill the ear and imagination with a felt-sense of a soundscape and bodyscape, where the human and more-than-human meet, merge, and entangle. Georgie creates timeless worlds, alive with multiple species and eros, each poem pulses – opening up and closing shut like a bud.

Anna Selby

First published in 2022 by Fourteen Publishing.
fourteenpoems.com

Design and typeset by Stromberg Design.
strombergdesign.co.uk

Proofreading and copy editing by Lara Kavanagh.
lk-copy.com

Printed by Print2Demand Ltd, Westoning, Bedfordshire, UK.

Georgie Henley has asserted their right to be identified as the author of this work in accordance with the Copyright, Designs and Patents Act 1988.

This book is sold subject to the conditions that it shall not be lent, resold, hired out or otherwise circulated without the publisher's prior consent. Any republishing of the individual works must be agreed in advance.

ISBN:
978-1-7391697-1-8

Amphibian

Georgie Henley

contents:

Encroach

I'm filled with things I'm afraid of
blood / love / ambition
32 teeth according to my tongue
people have called me brave
but I am simply able to tolerate pain
one day my father will realise I'm average
he sent me a card once
with a small girl on the front
singing with her mouth wide open
I fold it in my stomach, barren kangaroo
something for my ego to cling to
pray the next person who touches me
will leave it undisturbed
slender talisman
against the fraudulent dawn

Albatross

At seven days old, when your eyes stayed blue
and darkened a little, like your father's,
a tinge of sea-grey, did you feel it then?
The weight of something ten times your size
hanging from your neck, a carcass, heavy
feathered thing, the muffle of mighty wings
dragging in your shadow.

You grow taller, grow used to the burden,
even enjoy the pressure on your chest, each night
two bodies tucked under a shrewd moon.
You are chastised so many times your mouth grows dry,
each tap spouts saltwater, you must open your arm with spiked teeth
to moisten your tundra-tongue.

This is the way the world finds you:
salt crusting each pore,
salt the reek of want,
the heavy feathered desire.

You are schooled in humiliation,
slump against radiators to melt the ice slipped down your spine,
worry they can see the blood seeping from the beak
hooked at your clavicle.

You didn't know then, that sharpened flute of bone
could turn saltwater into fresh,
tears into nourishment,
that soon you would watch your skin
grow plump and new with each crisp disappointment.
On the other side of the world, you see a live one for the first time
nibbling the glossy crook of its neck and then in a flash
it glides skyward – godlike, buoyant.

How many times had you begged
to be shrived, to shed the hulking guilt?

How many times had you bitten
the insides of your cheeks, to stop a smile born of sin?

How many times had you set out on new seas
looking for new ground
only to return to yourself?
You see two bodies circling in the high blue air.
You see two lovers climbing in hope.

You hardly notice your chest made light, so glorious
is the soaring corpse, like a noble ghost, like all the ghosts
punished for their pride, made only noble in death;
exultant, its wingspan taut sails,
you think maybe that's what love can feel like –
the opposite of shame.

playground

I promise you I was
almost pretty, once
even though all my manners
are now stuck
in my throat, bound
up with old
honeysuckle,
as a girl, had everything:
striped dress succulent diction
red and green crocodile
hand in hand two by two
a locked gate larynx
and I carried a book
with a picture of a dragon
painted every colour
of an angry sky
watched all the lovely faces
split into spiteful little grins
they tried to rip out my pages
but they could not take my fire
and I would not let them win

bloodsport

she had a hound in her house
big brown dog, nose in my crotch
they can smell blood or fear or both

when we were twelve and her braces
came off, her teeth looked gigantic
and gorgeous and terrifying

that's when the hunt began
when she saw my flat chickened feet
and round cheeks turning red when I ran

for my life, hearing her behind me
laughing, gnashing her perfect teeth
smelling blood or fear or both

Partition

one of the blonde girls who wore cargo shorts always had
men coming out of her room
with arms so bruised you couldn't see
their new tattoos,
the first to heal was a lightning bolt
I asked him if he wanted one
when we walked one of those desolate American roads

it's freezing but regardless
I watch him lie down in the street
to prove something and I hesitate
because I am seventeen
and still confuse admiration and love and lust
in a fruit salad where everything tastes like yellow juice, youth

and sleeplessness, even though my bones rattle like a storybook parrot
I lift light flesh through the corridors
listen sometimes for sex,
read on the communal computer screen
that a director I like is making a film about
some creep in a motel;

on someone's birthday
there is the cool promise of night-swimming
after hours, pool shimmering
in the domed humid crush and the smell of quesadillas
coming from the kitchen next door
where I ate onion soup to please my mother,

that night, sat with the pack
laughed young and dumb, trying
not to watch her eat –
the new girl – forking scorching pasta
red enough to stain everything
and later she stripped down to her underwear

lowered herself into the warm blue and asked me
smiling, to get in
like she could hear me aching
her face was freckled and her armpits were dyed hot pink, like Cupid

blushing mischief,
like she knew that all the girls in my dreams had orange hair now
when her boyfriend came to stay
I waited outside their door one night
until my breathing became repulsive
hungry ghoul drifting, dreaming,
returning to a twin room
with an empty bed
with my mother sleeping next door
and the sound of her oblivious sighs
unaware of the luxury
of sharing a wall with you

Sim Theory

the daily itinerary is always the same: maintain your viridescence
it's nice here, someone else is responsible for everything
it takes less than two minutes to learn how to cook macaroni and cheese
and there is not a shred of yellow wallpaper in the house

she gussies up, shaves her head for the day
flounders when the taxi blares
does she lean her head against the window
does her hairline blur the glass

god is unwashed and selectively omniscient
this little body is simpler for now
maybe this would be the place
to encounter another 2-D soul, and eureka!

today her lover has quadrilateral plaits and sensible shoes
and it only takes four minutes of sustained coquetry
to move their mouths against each other
rake their fake flesh with dull claws

but god has a blue-light headache
watching love-bytes hurts her stomach
and her water glass has been empty for five short hours
above the sea of green diamonds, a ruby spilling blood

Gardenia Song

I have put the bouquet in the living room
on the table and they were drooping

I thought you would know what to do
but I couldn't ask so I have been watering them ludicrously

I have been laughing all day
can flowers have too much water

they have smartened up considerably though
they are falling out the vase

cascading, they are irrepressible, they are a new blush
these petals, leaving their heavy silk on my palms

I have forgotten the smell
or maybe I never knew it at all

I am opening the windows
I am hoping the sun will do something

I love my dreams you are so real and strong and
when I wake up I water the flowers

I have been watering the flowers all day, on and off
last week I lost my watering can and smashed something

please tell me if you see it
I know I take up some of your time

I imagine it as a gallery of binoculars
looking the wrong way

or a shard of lapis
playing good satellite

I have lost all your sounds too
and have been meaning to raise it

I'm quite suspicious you've been hoarding them
and placing them in the mouths of strangers

who then become friends I wish
you could meet everyone

the house is a fountain of flowers
and the cake and I bought candles too

although I'm worried to light a flame
the flowers are everywhere their noise is too loud

gardenias were they your favourite for the name
I know you are a word-lover

and I like you in a garden the picture of that
or more like a ranch, all white open skies

and a lake in sight to swim I cannot
promise you the sea even in my dream-making

but I know that some of her saltwater
still cries out for the weight of you

the flowers are in my mouth
is it better to speak or to die

I would like to send you an email
and wait for your reply

it was a beautiful home you built together
I'm sorry I couldn't go into the bathroom

I could hear the angel crying still
the tiles were too white
and they saw too much
the double Adonis cleaved in two

I wish you were here to help
the flowers are pouring from the windows

it is not a scent I ever asked to know
look how I water your loss look how it grows

Sell the Public Flowers

remember summer hot and proud and

unhurried, a promise of –

trying to concentrate at the Guggenheim

Mapplethorpe's flowers

are only your body your

body 1000 times your body

how can you drink whiskey with no trace of irony

later that afternoon I cover you

in calla lilies

the long stems too

every microscopic hair bristling my lips

insert an orchid in your urethra

leave the perineum unadorned

assume innocence

spontaneous poppied kiss

air smothered thick with ripened-black burst-open

figs, botanical asphyxia

why is everything gorgeous dangerous

I no longer remember your fragrance

only shame hot snake oil salesman

advertising the luxury of wet fresh delusion

Makeup Counter

she has bad skin and brown eyes
colour of burnt butter

and her grin is quick, it splits her face into
scrunched lids and cerise bright lips

the lipstick she paints me with
is *your perfect nude, with a touch of peach*

later I chew on my bottom lip
and pretend it's hot pink and hers

CIRCE i. swine-lover

lips cracking, mocked by the white-hot god
they hauled their panting corpses onto the shore

not believing their eyes when they saw her
arms and legs spread in starfished welcome

nipples wrinkled hard, ready
to receive them

belt of wild cucumber and vanilla pods clinking
they were delirious and unconvinced

until they heard her sing
the tobaccoed ripple of experience

she lay with them in the sand
fed them generously with her own arterial milk

red it was, and warm too
they were hesitant at first but

craved sweetness after months of salt
and later, when they'd stopped squealing

eyes pickled pearls blind
gleaming, bloodless, plucked so carefully

and kept dry in a green glass bottle
she caressed their swollen bellies

glowing mollusc in the candlelight
kissed each tearstained snout

crooning in quiet exultation
the birth of new sons

CIRCE ii. hero-lover

Before sometimes or after
I would assume the role of shadow, say –
let me take the weight;
press palms against the hinges of each shoulder
place a knee between your legs
and contract my elbows very gently
until I felt your knees buckle, breasts against your back,
your chest opening skywards,
the great exhale.

I've bathed most of my lovers
and listen to this, a half-secret:
I preferred it to the sex sometimes
when we would talk through our days
or other times be silent
except for the necessary questions –
is it hot enough for you?
do you need to wash your hair?

What is it about a soaking wet dick
growing hard in my hand
that makes me feel like I can
steer a great ship to safety,
avoiding every jagged tooth of rock
as conqueror, paragon –
is this what it feels like?
is this how you feel, all the time?

You wept, in Scheria, when they sang
your own story back to you,
perhaps you were angry
that beauty had been made from all that pain
and to remain a hero you hid your face
which is half your father's –
you don't need to do that here.
I soap your spine, tell you again
you are not your father.
When your voice breaks it is only the two of us who hear.

Be assured: they only know a moon of you.
Standing here, with your sun pouring over me
I pity them.
They have not felt the weight of stars.
I'll miss it, this bright possibility –
hearing the shimmer everywhere
like a soft low tide,
being able to reach out, touch
your glistening bones
and say come here
let me do that –
let me take the weight.

CIRCE iii. thief-lover

he loves many things about you
cries your body your BODY as he thrusts
laps your tang of sweat earth cunt
when you orgasm the scream blackens the moon
and it looks fabulous

in his homeland
they spit witch like it's a bad word
like it's not a gift
like they don't know you were chosen
remember when you listened to those dregs
how you had to unsex yourself
before you understood
you bled power

she's exceptional at weaving
and her armpits are impeccably bald
and you hate her because you'd probably be friends
from what he's told you
of her kindness, and firm disposition

he'll say you witched him
she-devil, scarlet girl
you lay on your back
and unfurled yourself
watermelon carcass
weeping with thirst
six-limbed
six-tongued
six-holed
necrowhore

he'd heard you could grow wings if necessary
begged you to show him
sometimes, you said, in my dreams

I scratch the down under my shoulder blades
and they surge from me
like pissing in a cold sea
I wish you could see them,
they bleed a little at the base
have you ever seen uncut tourmaline?

and you could tell he was disappointed
so soothed him in dovetalk
there's nowhere I need to fly
everything I love is here
and he gathered up your hair like a shining noose
later you'll tell yourself you knew just then
which is a false hex, what she'd call a lie

the day began like the other days
morning sex: dank-breathed decadence
then breakfast: sourdough, goat curds, redcurrant jam
then the morning loop:
you check the traps, pick grapes, snap a neck or two
you need some you-time
and he likes to stay in bed anyway, lazybones
he's growing fat and you love it
you return around noon, arms full
lips starved for his

and the gold is gone
and the boats are gone
and the sun is gone
and some epic poet will call him a hero
for leaving

Love Poem

do not underestimate what
a lonely woman will do
I am running my fingers over
the white piano keys
I am stolen with love for you
time waits for no ghost
but I am bruised with patience
the magnolia tree grows each night

stops the room with its dull yellow wax
roots muddling the bed
where fingers caress sand
a bridegroom of the ocean
merciless in her fitful void
there is no pity here amongst
the drowned and their undimmed glories
eyes left open to search amongst the reeds

the neighbours complain about the damp
lock their windows when they hear an animal howl

Blush

last night I met a girl
her smile was so wide
I dreamed she would
swallow me
a carnation in each cheek
I spread her sternum
ribs breathed heat
I have no heart only
hollow dragon husk
ravenous
I ache for what is golden
the source
I imagine how a bruise
a peony pressed
would bloom on her skin
fox blood in fresh milk
the hunger will kill me
before the thirst

The Sculptor

loves the skin off me
no hair no breasts, flesh
flayed into sacrilege
a single singing nerve
of wind-scored
blossoming verdigris
observe the perfect circle of my eye
this is honest work
this stark mercy
the tempering of blood

in her hands I am made
alien, god-touched
more than mortal
mutilated to beauty
hammer on chisel on stone on
rapture, sole witness to
the severity of her worship
her calloused rhapsody
kneading me into hillside
the wet yielding earth

she beholds me, gasping
unleashes the sore glorious sun

Killjoy

The laburnum trees are dripping yellow spoils.
When does spring stop being spring?
When flowers bloom into open mouths?

At a barbecue in winter I stick my hornet-stung finger
in the faces of my family, who are faceless and occupied.
I'm bored of carrying around my dreams
the morning after, like a glow-in-the-dark dog collar.
I'm bored of being a sullen itching warning.

I'll admit this is all wonderful material: the throbbing rhododendrons,
crenelated roofs, the Pinot Grigio abattoir where a laugh
is not really a laugh at all but a very thin knife
that twists in the evening's stomach.

It helps to call someone far away and retread my steps
on the barren field, wishbone goalposts scattered by the river
I dreamed of lying under in the middle of a ballet class.
The misted park glowing orange-green
like a badly lit sex scene.

I wish someone had told me that everything would be Vantablack
and then occasionally a vat of frozen lemonade shimmering,
to save me the anticlimax, of the split end travelling up the shaft
ready to splinter.

I should write more letters, and cut out hydrogenated fats,
and mend the holes in my old hairshirt,
but I won't do that.
I'll just dry-clean my old wool coat
and find a different place to hang it up
and pretend I am someone new and luminous.

The laburnum trees are dripping golden chains.
As if I needed something else to keep me tethered here.

Inhibition

it smells of lonely in here
and my cleaned-yesterday pussy

which is a word I used to loathe
before the ambit of my brain became

22 sanctioned walls
slipping between both hands

larger than a heart and discerning,
eel-slick, probably greyish

but I prefer to think it pink
and cool like fridge-frosted peaches –

the other night I had
a sudden urge

to spill pomegranate seeds
in my pubic hair

and let them hide a while
winking jewels in high resolution

itch scratched
scalp glowing

Today on Instagram

I watched 27 seconds
of a self-defence video
detailing how to protect yourself
in the event of being raped
and I felt stupid
it all looked so easy

Surveillance

it's rather simple a single bed and in the bin a dictaphone
whose clicks are being kind today and non-existent
which is really quite smug, to flaunt their silence

and not exist when they know it is my greatest aspiration
to smash through the glass and let my bloodied scraps be borne
away on a zephyr of cigarette smoke from the daddyboys swarming

outside the library, which looks like an asylum or a fascist bakery,
to get a good look, I've always been good at putting on a show,
a good window display

PARIS IS BURNING

PARIS IS BURNING and every angel is on fire
have you ever seen skin shine like that their
arms or their throats as they howl with joy
thank you for your exquisite faces
painted for the end of the world

PARIS IS BURNING and his planets are in freefall
Capricorns don't do well when their plans unspool
the palm reader was a bust she never
mentioned shame and now there's confetti
in his astronaut suit maybe he should
have worn lipstick there will be
no more red flowers in his lifetime

PARIS IS BURNING and the percentage of nylon
is the biggest concern and rightly so these suits
have been standing in front of the flames
for years now with timetabled water-breaks
if you've ever sat at Time's table you will know
that the seats are long-melted
their only view the irrevocable wave

Celebration

Dreadful: to be full of dread.
Too many ghosts.

I leave coins in the crooks of trees
for the restless dead.

On my birthday I receive salt
which I use to scrub the skin

I took off the night before.
You think it means something

to be given a name?
Next time we make love I will ask you

to scream blue sunrise and tell me again
I exist.

Dorian

bloodthrum of bass
dancer-body singing through
the tide of struggling flesh
graceful Midas grazing
every iris obliterated
lustdrunk burning
for him, beauty
in the eye of the beheld

and she, the seer
coked-up soothsayer
drapes a long arm
lily-skinned, gilded with shiver
between her fingers the petals
pressed, rubbed
burn her cool perfume
green-haired ingenue
arranging herself in corners
awaiting his hand to hook around her pelvis
his hot murmur that she is fascinating

the carved jaw in glass skin
cheekbones leonine, he catches
sight of himself in a black hole
a rabbit's bloated pupil
gets hard at his own echo
in someone's lime-tinted lenses
tastes a flash of prettyboy
twirling, gurning
buzzcut ballet, knuckles sparkling
he freezes, knows he vanished
common procedure

presses on, bares his mouthbones
sweet-talk eyelash dance

sees the pup's phone lockscreen
snorts in flattered disbelief
poor baby sniffs, stammers
I had to, you looked so...
granted he's not the first
and he won't be the last
but the kid's got a talent

he took him home last year
goldsmiths dropout
beautiful, lacking in basic hygiene
kept his rings on during
a fistful of silver

and after watched him smoke out the window
saw him turn, say
the light's good, let me –
clicks a quick pic
and gets back into bed to suck his cock
one last time, slowly until
mouth full, eyes shining he wonders
if this is how angels taste

he develops a reputation
hotshot, divine spooge
applies snail mucin essence
drinks nettle tea to regulate blood glucose levels
and reduce inflammation
googles aneurysms
redundant botox
watches scalps breathe crimson pixel

eye candy leaving
mouths empty
the unsatisfied masses ravished
by glory's parasite

the nose rots first, revealing
staring nostrils and bone
cheek muscle an unplucked cello string
the polaroid in the attic bleaching out
to nothing
white wolf stalks the moon
ghosting Death's fruitless kiss

Wish You Were Here

Paloma, tall blonde glass,
hums a little warmth.
It rains harder here,
you say – *this is how it rains in Las Vegas*
like great big god shits.

Two new virgins split the sky
over a power-station graveyard.
We pack up, head out

to look at dead robots in the sun
freshly drenched
and eight stone spider eggs
stored in a separate room to
their sprawling mother
standing impossibly
her body one huge heart
collapsing slowly under

the heaviness of love and humiliation
in early August,
you say – *you can have the figs*
then tomorrow, rush to other altars

proved unnecessary
by your torso stretched across dawn.
You play a Pink Floyd song,
you say – *this is one of the best songs ever written*
which means you've known this affliction.

We return to the city,
bones humming gold,
and every light is green.

Wordplay

I want to be very honest
in my capabilities that this is
only a poem and not my hands
in their everyday silver
I cannot reach out,
hold where your jaw
meets your neck, touch
the jut-hello of bent elbows
I am doing my best with words
and their limits I am listening
to the same song every hour
and finding new threads
in its cosmos, I would sculpt
your torso if I could
the sternum first in case
it is the only thing committed
to future relic, I would use
these hands for more than writing
more than praying if I could
I would like to know
their every use
your every bone

after the repeated loaning of ribs

I have stretched my hunger into a white canvas tent / people come to live in my want for a while / and its long days of desire / it is an anonymous hunger / it has made me a mapmaker of faces / I am able to be slaked by most rivermouths / with enough perseverance / we talk our carnivore talk / collect old birch, pine stumps / to burn outside / for the frightening heat, and discussing of perishables / after, I return inside the bright taut skin / collect salt in kingdoms / I like to see my hunger plain / a cave of throbbing bone / stubborn in the hot light

(casenotes on following the moon)

There is little gratification, you must become acquainted with elusion.

Remember that? Living thread to thrill to ache to dust, wooing the bright desolate ghost.

It is not a chase. It is not something to be caught, or captured by an inferior lens.

It can be many things, it can be:
a plate of white fish and plums for breakfast / knuckles on a gearstick, a test of self control / the outer iris line at the point of rhapsody (NB: on occasion art eclipses sex in this respect).

This is not a pursuit only reserved for nighttime. Consider the moon pale amongst pale skies above an athletic track, city water, the day's final blue and rose.

Mist helps. As does a sky scrubbed of stars in March.

There is no end, and you will forget how you began.

It may surprise or irk both companions and colleagues.

You might feel special. Resist this. There are many others committed to this undertaking.

It is not a competition. It is not a race. There will be no anointing of laurels. This is a quiet glory. And sometimes it will be sad and hard.

Expect disillusionment, no good thing is entirely clean. But know: this is closest. The necessary light. Watching and waiting, to find its kin in us all.

4.11

I undress differently for her
without shyness, bravery
as if I am alone
in the early dark-mauve, sometimes
she hides her face and it is
only her cool flare wild on my shoulders
her sure floodlight
thawing with hollow joy
perhaps tonight I will sleep
with my face turned towards hers
between us only the clear night
and our souls, at rest

the gloaming

I watch the light-show on
the backs of my eyelids

harlequin, diode white
citrine, the blue-dark

forever blurred galaxy
the aurora is pixelating

the retina
is highly light-sensitive

and now
the yearning tide

the heavy want
to surrender

to dream we enter
love's dark valley

Revolution

cool hands on wretched skin
puckered up, I did it myself
and I'm not proud
but the sea always arrives
with her annihilating kiss
and forensic tongue scanning sand
the hermit crab's untouched data

I see you standing there looking for heaven
a word that sounds very lovely
where the earth itches the same
a grain of sand is just chickenshit rock
stepped on and stepped on and
there is fake egg yolk
dripping down your skull

just in time for the shining catch
a haul of freshly shucked lusts
slit from scalp to navel
she's brazen with it, her daily glut of seawater
purges until she's sainted silver
sticks new pearls in her gums
and beams

***

time is told through our body
two glass hills, kitten-smooth
filled with feeble stones
trickier versions of their gaolers
urgent, inevitable
or our faces, moon-round
numbers carved just below the hairline
a mother-of-pearl complexion

your first morning off school was decided by the moon
what's between your legs keeps you up at night
a man lectures you on history
periodically sniffs the air for blood
tells you your mother should have had an abortion
I hate science, or anything said with certainty
too long tethered to unknowing, its sawtooth gizmo

yes I know the only good love stories happen in deserts
yet still surrender to broad river hands
be patient with me, I am trying to make sense
of the hot blue noise
I would like to grow happier, slowly
so I remember it and the whole evening
I will look like I just got off a horse

sometimes only jackals watch a ship sinking
murky with hope
the place between fever and sleep
where were my pack, my pact-sisters
unspooling our mythology of bones
we stopped sitting in circles
we broke the moon's clean line

one day it will become real
and have a colour that other people know the name of
surely there has to be more than
the cord pulled taut
the smug compass, a designated face
two weeks of monosyllables
rut after rut after rut

***

I am lying in the many-clovered grass
I am in the place between fever and sleep

fuck you and your big blue American sky
let me know when you have skinned your first shoal
hoisted it above your bedroom window
tender as cellophane and somewhere in its fog there is
your mother wheeled to the shower, exhausted by joy

the bath is growing cold
yesterday's fruit has new bruises
there's a failed romance on the corner, leaking meat juices
please remember the blossom strewing in drains
was a blessing to pay witness to
I open my wrists to the sea
an offering

for her toothless kisser
legs spread wide
and even then I will swallow the mouthful of old sand again
I know there was never an option to spit
remember again the lime on the rim of it all
welcome it again, and suffer it
fiercely, without question

Acknowledgments

With thanks to *clavmag* for publishing "Encroach", and to Hazel Press for including "ii. hero-lover" in their *O* anthology.

More thanks are due to Ben Townley-Canning at *fourteen poems* for publishing "Blush", and believing in *Amphibian.*

Finally, thank you to my queer family for introducing me to true freedom, and to my parents for their boundless love and support.